WRITING
A MINI-MEMOIR

WRITING A MINI-MEMOIR

how to create a book from your experiences, thoughts, family lore and customs

Alison Chisholm

First published in 2014
by Caleta Publishing

Copyright © Alison Chisholm 2014

ISBN   978-1-291-94474-7

Printed and bound by Lulu.com

WRITING A MINI-MEMOIR

It has never been easier to self-publish, and to create your own book. Print-on-demand publication has taken over from photocopied sheets attached with rusty paperclips. It has dispensed with the massive set-up costs that used to mean a project was only financially viable if you ordered and sold a hundred copies.

You don't have to plod around all the printshops in town in search of the best price. You compare companies online, and pick the one whose styles fit in with your vision for your writing project.

You may have an incredible story to tell, or vital life-lessons to communicate. You may simply want to collate the memories of a good holiday for your own interest, or share snippets about your childhood with other members of your family.

Whatever your project, you have complete control over its content and appearance, and the option to produce something absolutely private or available for the public to buy.

Enjoy!

CHAPTER ONE
WHERE TO BEGIN

People like to reminisce. Personal news exchanges include highlights from the last few days or weeks. Mention a recalled memory in company and someone will come up with a story on the same subject. Get the family together and tales of the Great Trifle Incident or the Amazing Vanishing School Report are fondly remembered. We are entranced by writing and reading facebook entries, twitter and blogs.

It's hardly surprising, then, that with the ease of e-publishing and print-on-demand, mini-memoirs have rocketed in popularity. These books are fun to write, absorbing to read, and they become a family archive to fascinate the next generations. If this final point sounds improbable, think of it the other way round. Would *you* be fascinated if someone gave you an account of your great grandparents' wedding day, memories of driving in the 1920s, or the fun of the village fair a century ago? If the answer's yes, writing a mini-memoir is a social obligation as much as a pleasurable activity.

Mini-memoirs can be developed into much larger volumes of autobiography, and if you want to write about your life in depth, they are a good way to experiment with different styles and formats, such as first and third person approaches, tense selection, and the personal style that constitutes the writing's register. If you are not sure about embarking on the full autobiography, they give you a taster to help you decide whether the genre is for you; and even if you change your mind about the longer project, you still have something to show for your work.

It sounds too obvious to suggest that the first requirement of a mini-memoir is to decide on its topic, but many attempts at the genre founder because their author has not defined the parameters of the book. Remember that this is a slice of life, not a whole life. If you don't already have a fixed idea of the ground you are going to cover, it's worth making two lists.

The first takes the form of a timeline, and although it may already be clear in your head, it's a good idea to note it down on paper. At the side of the page list either the years from your birth to today or your ages from 0 to now. Try to keep to one sheet of paper, for ease of looking back. Fill in key events in your life alongside the year or age, remembering that some years will be cluttered, others blank. You may end up with something like this fragment of a timeline:

7 Entered junior school Brownies Sister born
8 Chickenpox
9
10 First holiday in Wales Learned to play tennis
11 High School First experiment with nail varnish
12 Detention in physics Uncle died Music exam
13
14 First date New puppy
15 Moved to new town Teenage rebellion Trip abroad
16 Tonsils out Joined amdram group Row with best friend
17 Driving lessons Started work

You may find it helpful to mark the paper with lines linking the periods spent in different places, or doing different activities, eg. Brownies membership, attending particular schools, period of teenage rebellion could all span a number of years.

This may seem a rather tedious exercise, but it's amazingly helpful for writing quantities of mini-memoirs with different themes, and invaluable if you go on to write a longer autobiography.

The second list is not totally time based, but rooted in activities and places. Don't worry about chronological order, but cover your page with interests and slices of life. Everything from best or worst subjects at school, crafts, holidays, hobbies, places you've lived, jobs, periods of illness, relationships, vehicles you've owned, sports, club memberships, religious groups, political affiliations ... is grist to the mill.

Like the first list, this will take some time to compile, and both lists should be kept open for additions and adjustments to be made. There will, of course, be huge areas of overlap; but this is not a problem. Looking at the same information from different angles is stimulating, and the lists will feed off each other to build a more complete picture.

All the time you are working on your lists, your mind should be open to the potential for exploring different aspects of your life in a mini-memoir. This is useful even if you have already chosen a theme, as it demonstrates the opportunities for follow-up material. If you still have to choose, ask yourself what you would most enjoy writing about – it's as simple as that.

One special consideration that might influence your choice of theme is the question of how your writing will impinge on other people. If everything you say is provable truth, nobody can deny your right to say it. But if people you care about might be hurt or offended by your reminiscences, you may feel sensitive to certain subject areas.

If you remain spoilt for choice, work out which theme would have most potential for expansion. An account of a disastrous holiday could lead to a tragi-comic anecdotal book of holiday experiences. A description of the way your family celebrated Christmas when you were a child might prompt you to write a non-fiction how-to book about getting organised for the festive season, including information about recipes, pastimes, decorations, gift wrapping, etc. that you recall. A humorous tale of the trials and tribulations of learning to drive could inspire you to create a compilation book, gathering stories of lessons and tests from friends with information to share.

By thinking ahead in this way, you are not committing yourself to anything. You are just keeping some interesting options open.

If you are an experienced non-fiction writer, your immediate thoughts will be *What of the market research? Shouldn't I be writing what an editor wants rather than pleasing myself?*

The response is both depressing and liberating. It's depressing because, at the time of writing, the mini-memoir has very little commercial potential. You will probably have to be your own publisher and e-publisher, and – more difficult – your own sales force, your efforts assisted by online publicity. You are not likely to top the bestseller lists. In other words, please don't give up the day job.

The liberating side of the coin is that you are *not* beholden to anyone else. Editorial style, word count and presentation do not figure. You are going to create the project you want to see, in the way you want it to appear, that will showcase something about yourself. Relish that fact.

Up to now there has been a passing reference to a few possible themes for your mini-memoir. Let's bring some ideas together to provide a springboard in case you are still undecided.

- the job from hell
- living in a mobile home/high rise flat/different country

- happiest days? - memories of high school
- the summer I made a kit car/played golf/joined a choir
- when Santa came to our house
- my gap year
- facing the pirates/intruders/ghost
- family parties
- baby days
- flirting and dating

As soon as you have decided on your theme and its parameters or time boundaries, start putting together a hoard of material on which you can draw. This can be divided into three general areas: memories, mementoes and research.

Memories

The major inspiration for autobiographical writing is your own memories. If your heart sinks at reading this and you are anxious that your memory could let you down, don't worry. Give yourself time and try a few simple exercises, and you might be surprised.

Start with all the memories your theme produces without particular prompting. Let the thoughts flow, but jot them down. Even the most accessible can slip away when you are actually involved in writing the book.

Don't worry about the chronology of these preliminary notes. Once all your thoughts are on paper, you can juggle them and play with different orders.

Memories are sharpened when they are related to the senses, so try this exercise. Close your eyes for a moment and think back to one specific occasion related to your theme. (Closing the eyes gives you a clearer picture.)

First, remind yourself exactly what was happening at the time. Don't stop at *eating a meal on the train*, but recall that you were *on the route to Scarborough on a hot day and being served soup by a uniformed waiter*. Being more specific both helps with the clarity of your memories and gives you a reference point for research to fill in any blank areas. Yes, you can even Google the flavours of soup served in railway dining cars.

Next, question yourself on the sensory images you recall. What do you remember seeing, hearing, tasting, smelling and touching?

Move on to your emotional reactions. What emotions surrounded the memory in general? Were you happy, apprehensive, bored or excited at that precise moment?

A clearer picture should be building up. Boost this exercise with another to add still more clarity to the memory. This time, instead of concentrating on the senses, prepare a series of questions for yourself as if you were being interviewed in minute detail. No topic is too small for consideration. You could begin with questions like:

- ⅄ What was I wearing, and how did I feel in it?
- ⅄ Was I alone or in company? Who was with me? Why?
- ⅄ What was I carrying on the train?
- ⅄ What was the weather like?
- ⅄ If I was reading a book, what was it?
- ⅄ What do I remember about the stations on the route?

The more questions you formulate, the clearer the emerging vision will become.

You can add depth to the background of the incident by creating another list of questions which are not significant to the moment you're recalling, but focus on your lifestyle at the time. Start with these:

- How old was I?
- Where was I living?
- Was I working or in school? Where?
- What were my preferred leisure pursuits at the time?
- What sort of clothes did I favour?
- What were my favourite films/music/TV programmes?
- Who was closest to me?
- What made me angry?
- What was my most treasured possession at the time?
- What was my favourite food?

Again, the more you ask the more colour you will produce.

By the time you have worked through these exercises, you should find that the initial memories you jotted down have been enhanced and augmented. You might be startled by the quality of your recall, but there are still avenues to supplement your memories.

Mementoes

Even the slightest tendency to hoard pays dividends when you are writing mini-memoirs. If you are an inveterate hoarder, you have a massive advantage. Old letters, postcards, diaries, greetings cards and cuttings are pure gold as memory prompts and evidence of dates and places. Souvenirs and curiosities, ephemera, shells and pebbles, pressed flowers and leaves are practical reminders of times past.

More official documents, such as old passports, birth and marriage certificates, exam. certificates, school reports, medical documentation, etc. can help to 'fix' in your mind events alongside the background of your day-to-day life.

Perhaps the most valuable part of the hoard is the photograph. Snaps of celebrations and get-togethers provide immediate visual recall. Simply naming all the people in a picture brings memories of them to life and helps you remember the texture of any event.

You can create a list of questions to help you scrutinise the mementoes just as you did for the memories. As an aside, the answers to these can be intriguing and quirky. You might find they lead you on to write a 'freestanding' poem or filler based on the memento in addition to your mini-memoir.

Keeping all this material together in a box or life file ensures that you can top up the material stored in your head in an instant, giving extra information and depth. The 'together' is important. When you're writing, you will not want to have to search the house for that precious postcard whose message confirms something you want to include. Everything's to hand. If you want to avoid clutter, invest in a transparent storage box that can be stowed under the bed, or a stool or ottoman with a compartment for hiding all the bits and pieces in full sight.

Research

When you have exhausted all your own memories and hoards of mementoes, you can glean a lot more information for your mini-memoir by doing some research. The amount you do is your own choice. If research fascinates you, you may wish to spend hours with reference books or websites. If you find it the least interesting part of the project, a quick check where necessary can be accomplished in a few moments.

The research divides itself into two branches. You can establish direct facts and timescales, historical data and associated factoids, by using a search engine. If the facts are an essential part of your mini-memoir, make sure that you confirm them by checking a variety of websites or a reliable reference book.

A useful tip for adding general flavour to your writing is to study archive copies of the local newspaper for background. These may not contribute directly to your work, but will alert you to the concerns in the area at the time you are evoking.

The other type of research is more personal, and rooted in opinion rather than fact. This is the consultation research which adds new dimensions to your writing. All you need to do is seek out anyone who shared the experiences about which you're writing, and get their 'take' on the story.

People observe things differently, and remember different details. If you doubt the truth of this statement, ask someone in the police who has taken a number of witness statements to the same occurrence. It might seem as if everyone was watching a different event. Even basic points, such as the colour of a vehicle or approximate age and height of a person, can be recalled differently.

If you can get together with two or more people who shared your experience, simply get them talking about the event and they will spark each other off, reminiscing in more and more detail. Be prepared to prompt them with your own memories. Make plenty of notes/e-notes.

Take advantage of the assembled company to supplement your general background information. Starting a conversation about the times you shared will set a new chain of reminiscences tumbling into the chat. Again, make sure you write things down.

You may be alarmed by the variations in the material you gather. Your contacts may have no wish to mislead you, but as we have seen their memories may not be perfect and may be at odds with yours. Ask yourself how important 100% accuracy is. If the spirit of the occasion is more important than total accuracy, there's no problem. If you insist that every detail is right, you will need to concentrate very carefully on the information-assembling stage of the process.

CHAPTER TWO
GETTING IT WRITTEN

When you have fixed on the theme for your mini-memoir and assembled and sorted through all your memories, papers, pictures and research material, it's time to start the writing process. First you have to choose the style of your book. We'll look at four possibilities and some points to consider for each. Remember that you are in charge. You will choose the length, (often between 32 and 64 pages,) and scope of your book. You will pick the format and the cover, decide on its design and its price. When you've made your selection of style – just go for it!

Prose Narrative

A straightforward account of events is the simplest to organise and should flow easily and naturally, like a short story or novella. These ten tips are worth bearing in mind.

1. Be conversational. Formal writing is for reports and dry tomes. If your book is to fascinate its readers, its tone should be chatty and accessible.

2. Don't forget that appropriate sentence structuring, grammar and punctuation are a courtesy to the reader, and will give your book an air of polish without detracting from its conversational nature. If you have any anxieties in this area, you can find help online or ask a sympathetic friend to check your writing. As most mini-memoirs are self-published, it's unlikely that you will have a lovely sub-editor doing this part of the work for you.

3. Make your work reader-friendly by dividing it into easily managed chunks. If you don't want the formality of chapters in your relatively short work, you can break up the text by leaving a gap of a couple of lines where there's a logical break in the content. This allows the book to be put down and picked up conveniently, (in the unlikely event that readers will be able to put it down.)

4. Beware of excluding the reader. If your mini-memoir is to have a wider readership than just the family, in-jokes may need to be explained, and characters introduced by more than the name, eg. *John from next door* or *I'd known Louise since we started school on the same day.*

5. Avoid repeating yourself. We tend to repeat things in conversation to make sure a point doesn't get lost, but this is not necessary with the printed word or ebook.

6. Keep to the same person and tense structure throughout the writing. If you start with *It was on my eighteenth birthday that I fell down the stairs and ended up plastered in more ways than one*, (first person, past tense) it doesn't make sense to start the next paragraph with *So here she is, sitting up in a hospital bed and feeling rotten* (third person, present tense.)

7. Make sure that your writing is fluent and reads easily. Readers 'hear' your words in their head, and a smooth, clear delivery of them enhances the pleasure in the reading. Make sure you read your text aloud throughout the writing process, and you can listen for this ease of language.
8. Ensure that there is a logical route through the content of your mini-memoir. Don't dart about here and there following any number of fresh tangents. Keep it focussed, and – at this stage – keep the chronology in order unless there are clear signposts to any flashbacks or flashforwards.
9. Remember that ordinary fiction techniques enhance your mini-memoir. Good characterisation brings the people to life. Realistic dialogue can help to move the story forward. Always practising the familiar advice to *show, don't tell* will create an engaging account.
10. Above all, keep the writing interesting. The cardinal sin is to bore your readers. Bring light and shade into your account. Use humour to leaven the story. If at any stage in the writing you yourself are getting bored with the tale, stop, re-think, revise and – if necessary – scrap sections of your work. Only when it enthrals you, and fascinates your readers, will the piece be worthy of being launched on the public.

A well constructed prose narrative reads like a finely crafted piece of fiction, with careful pacing and a balance of content, so that appropriate emphasis is placed on each part of the account. It will grip the reader with both style and subject matter, making it a real page-turner.

You are aiming to leave the reader thinking *That was great – when's the next instalment coming?* This reaction, of course, gives you carte blanche to start on your next mini-memoir.

Poetry Version

If poetry fascinates you, it's interesting to use it as the format for your mini-memoir. You may still decide to follow a straightforward narrative line, and write your account as a single, long piece of poetry.

Verse autobiographies are nothing new. Wordsworth's *The Prelude* is an example, and a later poet laureate, John Betjeman, wrote a verse autobiography, *Summoned by Bells.*

Poetry's rhythms – and rhyme and metre if applied – give the writing a memorable quality, buttressed by the form's dynamics and use of language.

An easy form of poetry to use in order to create a mini-memoir is blank verse, which has proved an ideal medium for long poems through the centuries. Blank verse consists of any number of lines of unrhymed iambic pentameter, so that each line has five feet consisting of an unstressed followed by a stressed syllable.

Look at this example of the form from a poem about scuba diving, *Learning Salt*:

The simple act of kneeling in the sea
needs concentration, as her broad fins flap,
and weight of water pounds against her chest.
She breathes by suck and blow, her instinct bound
with lungs, must learn to trust by holding breath,
sweeping her mouthpiece out and back again.

She tries, and swallows brine. She chokes and splutters.
At last, mouth clogged with salt, she manages.

The language used in a blank verse poem can be immediate and contemporary, and the pattern of stressed and unstressed syllables reads naturally.

Stanza divisions are optional, and stanzas do not have to be of equal length. Blank verse poems often have stanza breaks only at the end of a section of content.

If you were writing a few hundred or even a thousand lines of blank verse, its pattern would soon become tedious. You can avoid this by including examples of the major variants of the form:

- the feminine ending, where an additional, unstressed syllable appears at the end of the line, demonstrated in the seventh line of the example.
- initial trochaic substitution, where the stress order in the first foot of the line is reversed to give a stressed syllable followed by an unstressed one. (The second and subsequent feet return to the regular pattern of unstressed followed by stressed.) This appears in the sixth line of the example.

In such a lengthy project, you may decide to break the text up occasionally by introducing a paragraph of prose, or a brief extract in a different form of poetry. Any variant should be applied at your discretion. If it works and reads well, leave it in. If it jars and 'shouts' at the harmony of the project, cut it out.

Blank verse is not, of course, the only option for your long poem. Ballad stanza works well in the narrative voice, using the familiar pattern of four lines in the stanza, the second and fourth of which rhyme. In its standard form, there are four iambic feet in the first and third lines of the stanza, three in the second and fourth.

Using the content of the example above, we can tweak the pattern to demonstrate ballad stanza:

The act of kneeling in the sea
    becomes the dive's first test.

She struggles with her clown-shoe fins
  as water pounds her chest.

Her lungs draw breath by suck and blow.
  She takes the mouthpiece, tries
to hold her breath, remove, replace;
  Salt clogs her mouth, her eyes.

This pattern can continue for any number of stanzas. It's also effective for humorous narratives.

Free verse is another good medium for your account. This has no specific metrical or rhyming requirement, which makes it easier to communicate a precise message without having to compromise the wording to fit in with rhyme and metre.

To work in free verse as distinct from chopped-up prose, the poem benefits from two points of technique. One is lineation. Check that lines end on a significant word, rather than something less substantial such as *in* or *of.* Try not to leave awkward phrase breaks at the line end. For example, there's awkwardness in:

The simple act of kneeling in the sea needs
concentration, as clown-shoe
fins flap, ...

The phrasing is more sympathetic in this version:

The simple act of kneeling in the sea
needs concentration, as clown-shoe fins flap, ...

The other point is the inclusion of slant rhyme, sound similarities appearing at any point in the line, that can help the writing to cohere as a poem. Plenty of examples of this add to the sense of poetry. See how many are used in the free verse version of the example:

> The simple act of kneeling in the sea
> needs concentration, as clown-shoe fins flap,
> weight of water pounds against her chest.
> She breathes by suck and blow, a primitive response
> to lungs' vacuum, must learn to trust by holding breath,
> sweeping her mouthpiece to arm's length and back.
>
> She tries, swallows brine, fumbles, splutters air, tries again.
> At last, mouth clogged with salt, she manages.

There are several examples of assonance, such as *kneeling/sea/ needs*, *clown/pounds*, *fumbles/splutters*, *clogged/salt*. Alliteration occurs in *fins flap*, *weight of water* and *kneeling/ needs*, while there's consonance in *against/chest* and *breath/ length*, and full consonance in *concentration/clown*. The repetition of *tries* and crossed syllable rhyming in *vacuum/ back* add another effect.

If you like the idea of working in poetry but feel that a single, long poem is rather indigestible as a mini-memoir, why not write a sequence instead? This features a series of poems which may stand alone but work best as parts of the major work.

Here each aspect of your account can be a separate poem. You may choose to write all your poems in the same form, such as a sequence of sonnets, or select different styles for them. It helps to have a pattern running through your work. You might create a chronological story, taking, for example, the events of a single day as the theme for your mini-memoir. This gives you the obvious opportunity to follow the timeline. You might follow a more lateral pattern, with poems about all the characters involved at the start, then a little narrative, some descriptions of background, a nostalgia piece, something more philosophical ... the choice is yours.

Compilation Piece

Maybe the easiest way to produce your book is to get plenty of other people to write the mini-memoir for you. Many people – family, friends and acquaintances – are more than happy to contribute to your project.

This is how it works. Suppose your book is to be about the period of time you spent in a particular job. As long as you are not going so far into the past that it's difficult to get in touch with former colleagues, rope in all the people you worked with and get them to provide your content.

All you need to do is to contact everyone you can, explain the parameters of your mini-memoir, and then ask if they'd like to contribute stories about you and your contemporaries, information about the hierarchy of the workplace, any publishable background material, working practices, etc. They should be willing to assign copyright in this material for your purposes.

If you give guidelines about your requirements, you have the chance to request specific material under a number of headings. This both gives you more work on which to draw, and gives you a better opportunity to use something from every contributor. It can be awkward if you solicit material from old friends and then don't get anything you can use. If each has offered you three or four extracts, you can usually find something worth including.

Give them some ground rules, such as all material to be typed or emailed, humour to be included where possible, and so on. Don't forget to give them a deadline, or there could be some unhappy contributors who see the mini-memoir in print before they've got around to sending their offerings. Remind them that you will have editorial control over the finished book, and that what you say goes.

In case anyone sees your book as the perfect outlet for venting opinions about the boss, it's worth reminding contributors that libel is a serious business, and if they can't provide proof of their accusations, they could be in trouble.

If your mini-memoir is more family orientated, it's a good idea to get the clan together just as recommended for research purposes. Invite as many family members as you can, your nearest and dearest as well as the ones who remind you that you can pick your friends *but* ...

It would be delightful to let the conversation flow and gather gems here and there, but that process may be too random. Tell them all when you ask them to come that they've been invited to have their brains picked on the subject of house moves/childhood holidays/the day the car broke down in Piccadilly Circus/the way your family celebrated birthdays – or whatever. Then they will arrive with appropriate memories and possibly old photos or other mementoes.

This is where you deviate from the research-collecting practice. After the conversation, laughter, recriminations and general banter, assign a specific writing task to each of them, relevant to the material they have brought to the gathering. If the occasion seems a bit stilted, ask them to email their stories to you. If it went well, you could plan to repeat the process in a couple of weeks, when everyone brings their contribution to be read and shared.

Not only does this produce another get-together, but it gives the opportunity to fine-tune both the quality of writing and the accuracy of content. It gives you, the compiler, a chance to hear the material and work out what needs amending, or how to juggle the order of contributions for best effect.

Another huge advantage of meeting like this is that everyone is made aware of the stories that will enter the public domain. You could even tell the assembled company that this is their last chance to censor anything they don't want to have shared.

Even with family, ground rules are important. The approximate length of each contribution should be decided, or you could end up with either a three volume novel or the contents of a postcard. Advise everyone of the house style you're looking for, so that you don't get some contributions written from the viewpoint of *I* in first person singular, others with *we* in first person plural, and others using *they* in third person.

Insist that you have editorial control over all matters concerning the finished book. This gives you the opportunity to correct your brother's misplaced apostrophes without drawing attention to them, create full sentences out of your aunt's brief notes, and clean up your granny's more salacious stories. It also means that you don't have to refer back to the other contributors repeatedly, but can go ahead and impose your own personal stamp on the writing.

When you have collected everyone's contributions, your job is to confirm their order, edit the copy, and provide linking material. The level of your own input is your choice. If the book needs little more than a few sentences to hold it together, mutter a prayer of thanks and go ahead with it. If the contributions are destined to be only a tiny percentage of the writing, charge up the laptop and flex your fingers ready to produce the rest.

If people – colleagues, family or whoever – have helped you with your work and given permission for you to use their words, they should be given credit. Let them know whether that will take the form of an author credit, eg. *Written by the Smith family, and compiled by Matthew Smith* or an acknowledgment of each contributor by name in a foreword.

It's a good idea to give contributors some idea of the expected date of publication. Always give yourself a bit of latitude. If you expect to complete the work in three months, tell them four. Contributors are thrilled when the book arrives earlier than expected, disgruntled if it's late.

Collage

Perhaps the most interesting format for a mini-memoir, from both the writer's and the reader's point of view, is the collage piece. This does not rely on a single form of writing, but brings together a pot pourri of styles. It can include:

- narrative, with straightforward passages of prose.
- short passages of comment and asides.
- jokes and anecdotes, relevant to the story but not embedded in the prose narrative.
- dialogue, presented as you would format a play, with character names alongside the words they say. If you are putting words into the mouths of living people, it's a good idea to run the dialogue past them first for approval.
- poems.
- diary entries.
- lists and notes.
- letters and other messages. (See note below)
- random curiosities or factoids.
- fillers and articles.
- timetables.
- hints you picked up along the way that might be of interest to other people.

Note: remember that letters, postcards, messages and other material written by somebody else are their copyright. You are the owner of the piece of paper the words are written on, but the ordering of the words themselves belongs to the writer. Most people are happy for you to quote from their work in the context of a mini-memoir, but you need to have their permission first. It's perfectly all right to quote from something you have written in a letter or card and sent to another person, of course.

On the subject of copyright, don't forget that you cannot simply cut and paste material from websites to use. There is no copyright on facts, but it exists on the wording that relates the facts. You are at liberty to reproduce facts in your mini-memoir, but make sure that you deliver them through your own words.

Collecting this type of material together is a fascinating practice. You can take your time over it, sifting through snippets and artefacts from a range of sources; or make a list of your mini-memoir requirements and set about assembling them all at once.

Because there are so many separate sections, you can complete a part of the book even if you only have a few minutes to spare on it. A single sentence factoid, tiny verse or briefly related anecdote might take no more than five minutes of your time; but you feel you have added something significant to your writing.

One possible problem with this scattered approach is that you could lose scraps of paper with information on. As soon as you realise you've lost something, it assumes massive (and probably disproportionate) importance. You believe the finest gem in the book has gone for ever. Avoid this by being meticulous about keeping all your material together. If you make use of pockets of time to work when you're away from your desk, cultivate the habit of carrying a specially designated notebook everywhere so that all your jottings are kept together.

The best part of a collage mini-memoir is working out how to assemble it. You might take a wholly random approach, but it can be useful – both for yourself and your readers – if you have some sort of direction through the work. It might be chronological, divided into cohesive groupings of information, or even alphabetical; but it keeps you on track and shows your readers there's a safe and controlled hand at the helm.

Whether you have a route or decide to use a freer layout, take time in placing the snippets into the pattern of the book, as you would fitting together the pieces of a patchwork quilt. A pleasing array of colours, textures and moods adds to the enjoyment.

There is no need to consider chapter or passage breaks to make this sort of book reader-friendly, as they are already present in the way the material is delivered.

When you have arranged all the pieces you've managed to gather, you will easily spot the areas where more (or less) input is required, where it would be useful to introduce better contrasts of style or format, and whether linking material is needed. As ever, reading the work aloud will guide you into the most attractive means of communicating your mini-memoir.

When you are preparing a collage piece for publication, one option is to use a different typeface for different sections of the book. Experiment with the appearance of the print, and select a range of your favourite typefaces.

You might use a specific typeface for all the narrative sections, another for diary entries, a third for verse, a fourth for anecdotes, another for factoids, etc., or take a more random approach. Just avoid the print styles that are difficult to read at a glance, such as those that look like handwriting or have contorted characters.

The Easiest Option

If you like the idea of producing a mini-memoir but still have any anxieties about the genre, the best place to start is with an experience that is self-contained and separate from your everyday life. This presents its own boundaries and yet gives plenty of scope for you to write.

The perfect example of this is an account of a holiday, the beauty of which is that you can start from scratch and create a deliberate hoard of material for a collage piece as the holiday passes. So the information gathering part of the mini-memoir is done for you, assembled, and will wait to be dealt with at a convenient time.

Provide a notebook for your material, and you can start filling it in as soon as the tickets are booked. Jot down departure times, packing details and so forth, but keep these in note form.

A word of warning: the pre-holiday material is the least interesting. Nobody wants to read a three-page essay on how you folded your clothes for packing, but they might be interested in the fact that you spent a week sorting out what you'd take and completely forgot to pack a pair of shoes. In other words, the ordinary merits a passing mention at the very most, but anything unusual or quirky deserves a little more attention.

As soon as you arrive at the destination, the interest level soars, and remains high until you set off for the journey home – which tends to be even more yawn-inducing than the pre-holiday content.

During the actual vacation you can keep a diary of names, places and events, with plenty of comment and particular notes of funny or unusual happenings. Add information you learn about your destination, and a separate note about the history and/or mythology of the place.

If you like people-watching, record your thoughts about fellow guests. Just make sure they are not mentioned by name (or identifiable) if you're making up curious lives for them.

Keep your eyes open for unusual sights, anything from the live chicken waiting in the bus queue to the menu that lists 'jacked potatoes with feeling', the road sign that indicates the same destination on two opposite routes at a roundabout, and the tiger cub being carried across the public square in someone's arms.

Look for different outlets when you're away, such as a shop selling nothing but Easter decorations throughout the whole year, a restaurant operating its menu in the format of a league table, where meals are promoted, demoted or relegated depending on how many people select them, or the market stall where you can have a massage in the middle of the shopping (and in the middle of the crowd).

Get into conversation about the places you visit. Find out that all the hotel's pictures were painted by a local artist, or that the shopping centre is built over the remains of a historical site, or that the bar is haunted.

Don't delay in bringing your notes up to date with everything you've observed, even the things you don't believe have much potential. Sometimes a small aside can be the perfect means of adding a touch of colour to a passage, and the minutiae can vanish if you don't write them down.

If you go on any guided tours, be sure to note down material from the commentaries. A fascinating snippet you could never forget can lose itself under the weight of the next half dozen points of interest.

As well as recording all the information, keep a collection of bus tickets, leaflets, maps, adverts, and any other documents you come across. Above all, take pictures of everything. This type of book cries out for illustration by photograph or line drawing.

All this may sound more like a school project than a holiday. The more you get used to the note-taking, the more efficiently and easily you will do it. Then when you get home, you have a terrific store of material from which to tease the contents of a mini-memoir based on your time away.

The added bonus is that you will be able to enjoy the holiday all over again while you are shuffling and playing with the material you are going to include.

CHAPTER THREE
FINISHING TOUCHES

As with any other piece of writing, putting down the final words marks the beginning of a new phase in the task, rather than the end of the work. It's time to go through it page by page, word by word, to make sure that every part of the mini-memoir is as good as it can be.

You are permitted a little break before you start this work. Indeed, some time off is recommended. It's hard to be objective about the oeuvre over which you have sweated blood in the past month/s. Distancing yourself from the toil of its creation, even if only by a week or two, allows you to return to it refreshed and ready to look at it with a degree of objectivity.

Begin by reading the whole piece through, preferably in a single sitting or at least on the same day. That's the beauty of a mini-memoir – it can be devoured in one go. Be as critical as your most discerning reader. This is your opportunity to get it right.

This overview of the book gives you the chance to see whether the idea that fuelled it has produced interesting enough content in general. If you, its author, find the account fascinating, then there's no problem. If it engenders a reaction of *So what?* you may need to re-think the piece.

A total re-think, though, is not inevitable. Maybe the concept of the book is good but its execution needs attention.

It's easier to re-work the whole book than to start from scratch on another topic. So check that you are still happy with your theme, launch yourself once more into the writing of it, and put the extra labour down to experience.

Maybe there are excellent passages but there's also some dross. A few judicious cuts can be made, leaving excellence with gaps. Filling in the gaps with new, more sparkling material is easier than a complete re-write.

If you do find that much re-writing is necessary, repeat the delaying process with the new version, leaving it aside for a while – at least a week – before you start to analyse it. Then take a day and read the whole script through, remaining aware of your reactions to the new version. Don't be tempted to skimp on this work and read only the passages that have been altered. The way the new text has been embedded is important. There's a risk that the finished book could be jerky and splitting at the seams if you don't reconsider your mini-memoir as a whole.

When you are happy that the content will hold the reader's interest, it's time to consider the more pedestrian aspects of revision. This 12-point checklist may help.

1. Have you remembered the suggestion to make your writing appear reader-friendly? Are there massive chunks of material to be got through, or is the text divided up into digestible paragraphs/stanzas/sections to welcome the reader?

2. Is the balance of the story working? Sometimes this can slip by unnoticed during the production of the piece, but it's important to make sure the most significant passages are given the most attention. Imagine a mini-memoir about a wedding day. Suppose there were forty pages. You would create an imbalance if you devoted thirty to getting ready for the occasion and the other ten

to the service, guests, reception, DJ, dancing, evening et al.

3. Have you covered all the ground you wanted to consider? Are you aware of an uncomfortable omission?

4. Have you said too much, and travelled into realms you would prefer not to have made public? It isn't too late to backtrack.

5. Focus on the technique of the writing. Although it is acceptable to make occasional deviations from standard syntax, grammar and sentence structuring, these should be done only to create a special effect. Is the bulk of your writing in properly crafted sentences, with appropriate grammar and punctuation?

6. Check your choices of vocabulary. Have you used the best word – on every occasion – to communicate the essence of your message? Does the wording seem over-simplified, pedestrian, or flowery and affected? Most mini-memoirs work best when the wording is straightforward and conversational.

7. Have you made interesting use of the devices of literature, such as similes and metaphors, irony, personification, flashback and so on?

8. Have you brought colour into your writing by including a few – but effective – adjectives and adverbs, and carefully chosen verbs?

9. Recalling the memory prompting exercises, colour can also be added by making good use of imagery, with references that relate to the senses. By describing sounds, smells, tastes and so on, you are introducing elements which are immediately recognised by the reader.

10. Is your writing specific and precise, or general and abstract? The specific is more convincing and appealing. Describing a person as *beautiful* is not

nearly as effective as mentioning their *emerald eyes and full lips*.

11. Have you introduced any conflict, one of the fiction techniques that can work really well in a mini-memoir? This doesn't mean you have to catalogue every argument, but that it helps to show opposing views and thoughts from time to time.

12. Does the writing appeal to the emotions? However interesting the content of your mini-memoir may be, it needs to bring emotional reaction along with account.

Don't forget that this is your project, you are in charge, and there is no need to rush. Take your time, looking at the elements listed above and any other possible problem areas.

Make any adjustments you wish, and then put your work away for a while. Repeat the process of revision followed by a resting period as many times as the writing needs. As a rough guide, wait until you have re-read your mini-memoir on two consecutive occasions without wishing to alter a word of it. Then it's ready for the next stage.

CHAPTER FOUR
GETTING INTO PRINT AND E-PUBLISHING

When your text is ready to meet its public, you can begin the exciting task of creating the actual book. The easiest way to do this is to follow a print-on-demand route, bearing in mind that the scope for producing a commercially published mini-memoir is almost non-existent.

Any venture into self-publishing is exciting but with just a tinge of anxiety attached. As well as being the perfect outlet for the mini-memoir, self-publishing is now embraced by many authors who want to take control of their publications. There are two major drawbacks, one artistic, one practical.

A self-published book is not subjected to the rigours of editorial control. It is up to you to ensure the writing reaches the very highest standards of crafting and professionalism. If you have the slightest doubts about your mini-memoir, you can buy in editorial services, or find a good friend you can trust implicitly to critique your work for you.

Self-publishing means that you are responsible for all your own sales. If your project is for sharing beyond the confines of a few friends and family members, you will need to be able to sell it yourself, via your own efforts and online.

One of the most established companies for print-on-demand books is the online publisher Lulu.com, so this is the example we shall follow through its various stages. It is always worth checking other companies when you are preparing a project, to ensure that the quality of the book and production costs are appropriate.

The first task is to register on the company's website, and then opt for a publishing project. You will be invited to select from a range of book sizes and shapes. Depending on your choice, you will then download a specific template, and drop your work into it. An A5, perfect bound version is easy to manage, and can be used for any mini-memoir of 32 pages or more. (The upper limit is 740 pages, just a bit beyond the scope of the mini-memoir.)

At the start of the book, you will need to supply certain pages you might not have thought about while you were writing. To see how other writers deal with these prelims, simply look at a few published books and you will get some ideas.

A simple guide is to put just the title on the first, half-title (recto) page, and leave the back of that page (verso) blank. The next recto page, the title page, may have the title with a little explanation, and the author's name. The following verso page contains all the 'official' information, including:

- ⅄ the publisher's name and year of first publication. It's good to have an appropriate and original name for yourself as publisher, and makes your enterprise look more professional. You don't need a clever logo, just come up with a name that suits you.
- ⅄ copyright symbol © with your name and the year.
- ⅄ assertion of your rights to the work, including the moral right of your recognition as author and details that limit other people's use of the work. The term 'All Rights Reserved' is often used.
- ⅄ the ISBN, or international standard book number. This is unique to your book, and ensures that it can always

be traced. Lulu.com provides you with an ISBN free of charge, which saves a lot of time, trouble and expense.

⚔ the printer's name and address.

The layout of this page varies, but the essential factors are the first year of publication, author's name and copyright symbol, and assertion of rights.

The recto page facing this may have a dedication, brief foreword or other peripheral matter, or may show a list of contents.

The verso is usually left blank and then … wait for it … the book begins!

The first page of the book tends to be the first page that's numbered, if you are providing page numbers. Numbers are implied on the prelim pages even though they are not shown, so the first page of actual text is often page 7.

Once you have placed the prelims and started the numbering process, it's time to examine the appearance of the content of each page. Think about your preferred typeface. You have probably already addressed this question if you are taking the collage approach, but if you have not, it needs some consideration.

Your template will have a default typeface such as Garamond in place, but this can be altered. As a point of reference, the book you are reading uses Times New Roman for the text, and the size is 12 point. Chapter and section headings are in Arial using the bold setting at the same size. The title on the half title page is in Arial 28 point, and on the title page Arial 18, both in bold. Additional information on the title page is given in Times New Roman, italic and roman, in 18 point.

At the end of each chapter, you should insert a page break, so that the positioning of the next chapter will not be affected by any alterations you make.

The next stage is to include photographs and drawings. Colour photographs will create a beautiful book, but these will add a considerable amount to the price. Just as an example, a 56 page mini-memoir published in 2014 in the form of an A5 perfect bound paperback is priced at £2.25 per copy to the author, containing black and white photographs. The same book with the photos in colour costs £8.61. (These prices do not take any postage and packing charges into account.)

The colour version is perfect as a gift for a special occasion, but rendered too expensive for its length to be sold to the public. There are small reductions for bulk orders, but not sufficient to make the colour printed book commercially viable. For general sales, the black and white version is used, with a note in the book of a website on which colour versions of the pictures included, and a few additional photographs, can be viewed at no charge.

In order to add photographs to the text, they must be saved on the computer and imported into the document as follows:

1. click where you want to insert the picture.
2. on the 'Insert' menu, point to 'Picture' and then click 'From file'.
3. locate the picture you want to insert.
4. double click the picture.

Your own line drawings, facsimiles of handwritten notes, etc., can be introduced into the text similarly as long as they have been saved as image files on the computer.

Artwork on the internet that has been designated for public domain use can be downloaded and saved on the computer, then inserted as above. Make certain, though, that this material is definitely freely available, and you are not infringing anyone's copyright.

Once you have set the fonts and placed any photos or artwork, it's necessary to go through the template page by page to ensure that there is a sympathetic pattern to the printing. If, for example, a title appeared at the bottom of one page and the passage to which it referred started at the top of the next, you would re-work so that title and passage were both on the same page. If a chapter ended with two words sitting alone after a page turn, it might be worth adjusting the wording slightly to trim the text so that the chapter was completed by the bottom of the page.

These cosmetic changes are worthy of your attention. They will make the book look finished and professional.

There is usually some white space at the end of the book, with a page or two of blank endpieces. Sometimes the number of pages required automatically produces these extra blank sheets, but if your text happens to finish on the final page you may wish to add a couple for a more professional look. They are generally not numbered, so you might have to remove the numbering from them. Numbers are removed by placing a text box over the area where they appear.

The completed book can be uploaded into your project area of the print-on-demand website, where it will wait while you produce a cover.

The website offers several styles of cover, and will give you the opportunity to change the colour and adjust the size and shape of its text boxes. Here the colour comes free, and you can include your photos without incurring extra cost.

The title, subtitle if used, and author's name can appear in a box on the front or printed straight onto the cover picture. If the book is large enough to have a spine, this can also be printed with the title and author. It's possible to add a note on the back of the book, and many of the cover designs allow for an additional small picture there too.

When you have played with the cover design and are happy with the picture, you can move on to the next stage and have a copy of the book printed. Just the one. It's tempting to take advantage of bulk order discounts right at the start; but all sorts of tiny problems of presentation can arise. These can be corrected in a few minutes, alongside any alterations you decide would benefit the text, and a second proof copy ordered. Assuming the second copy has no mistakes, you can bulk buy with confidence. (This advice is heartfelt, and comes from one who was over-confident and bought 100 copies of a book with tiny, barely legible print. Definitely a false economy!)

When your print version is in place, you can easily turn your mini-memoir into an e-book. Lulu.com provide a 21 page how-to manual explaining this, and it can be done without any cost to yourself. The e-book is compatible with all the major readers except Kindle, for whom you publish it separately through Amazon using Kindle Direct Publishing. Again, this is free of charge, but the publication system is slightly different, so you need to download their guide *Building Your Book for Kindle*.

If the whole business of putting your mini-memoir into book and e-book form seems too daunting, you can buy in a service that will do the job for you; but it's really very easy. With a little time and patience you can do all the work yourself, and then the labour of love that created the text merges with the creativity that crafts the book. Nothing beats the feeling of holding a copy in your hand, and knowing you did the lot, and that your own skills have led to every stage of the production of your book.

CHAPTER FIVE
THE LIFE OF YOUR MINI-MEMOIR

The book is in your hands. Your project has come to life. Where to now?

If your mini-memoir was only intended for the favoured few to read, it might be enough to purchase half a dozen copies and distribute them to the relevant people. If you want to take things a stage further, you will need to have a sales strategy. Start with a list of possible outlets, including:

- local bookshops. It might even be possible to organise a launch event here if you are on good terms with the manager.
- craft and gift shops, with eclectic stock.
- outlets connected with the content of the book. If you have written about experiences in a tennis club, for example, your local club might be willing to take some books. If you've focussed on your relationship with a church, they may have a bookstall.
- your social media contacts. Publicise your project on Facebook or in your blog, giving details for purchasing copies directly from you. Don't forget to factor in the cost of postage when you provide the information.
- craft fairs and sales, where you could hire a table from which to sell the books.

When anyone other than yourself is involved in selling the mini-memoirs, it's important to keep in touch with them, ensuring that they have enough stock and that you are on top of invoicing and collecting payment.

Don't forget to look at your online presence from time to time. Encourage people to buy through Lulu themselves or other websites, and your profile grows with each purchase and review.

The Personal Touch

One of the most interesting ways of publicising your book is on the public speaking circuit. If you want to sell copies and the information in the mini-memoir is of general interest, you can devise a talk based on it to deliver to interested groups.

Some authors find it daunting to give talks, but for many it's an added bonus to the writer's life, a source of new contacts, a little extra income, and a fascinating sideline.

If you are planning to embark on a public speaking career path, first you need to be sure that your topic will be of interest. Suppose your mini-memoir is about a holiday. A travelogue of *My Visit to Cairo* with the dreaded subtitle *A talk illustrated by 400 slides* is unlikely to find any takers. But if you could adapt your account to *Things You Need to Know when Sitting on a Camel* and substitute funny comments and one-liners for the slideshow/powerpoint demonstration, so much the better.

If you plan to speak only on your home territory, your nostalgic mini-memoir about growing up in the town everyone knows will have terrific appeal. The same book could be adapted into a talk with wider appeal if you simply held back on the local references, and talked more about the social history of the time on which you're focussing.

Should you be new to public speaking, or if this is a new topic to add to your repertoire, there are a few points to remember:

- ⚔ everyone is there to be entertained. The worst thing a speaker can do is bore the audience. What you say has to be fascinating, and the way you deliver it must be compelling.
- ⚔ when you're adapting your mini-memoir into a talk, you are not just reading the book. Your tone should be similarly conversational, but with plenty of asides and extra information. You can encourage some audience participation, and then when everyone's totally engaged in your material, let slip that you have written a book on it and happen to have a few copies with you …
- ⚔ you should practise your talk over and over until you could deliver it in your sleep – but also practise sounding spontaneous, so that your audience believe you've only just put the words together and are speaking them for the first time.
- ⚔ be careful not to rush. Although you are looking for a conversational approach, your speech should be a little slower and rather louder than your normal speaking voice.
- ⚔ keep your words alive with vocal variety. Be aware of variants in the pitch and speed of your voice, and don't be afraid to use pauses, both for dramatic effect and to allow you a fraction of a moment in which to gather your thoughts.
- ⚔ plan an organised route through your talk, so that your listeners know they are in safe hands being guided through the material you are communicating. You can even signpost the route, by explaining at the beginning that you're going to start with a bit of your childhood history, move on to talk about your foray into local

politics, and then look at the present situation in the town. You can refer back to the route whenever you make a transition from one passage to the next, by saying something like: *so much for my teenage years here. Before I was twenty, I'd decided to stand for the council* ... The audience at once remembers that from the plan. You could even add: *so much for my teenage years, and you can see why I've written a book about them.* It could make another sale.

⅄ if you are happy to field them, encourage the audience to ask questions. It builds up the rapport between speaker and listener.

When you have built your mini-memoir into a talk and practised saying it aloud until you are confident in its delivery, the time has come to start taking bookings. You will need to let the general public know about your work.

Start by using the word of mouth approach. Let it be known to interested parties that you have a talk to give and explain its content, and ask would their club/retirement home/U3A group/writers' circle/school etc. like to have you as a visitor? Spread the same information via your library or a register of local speakers, and see if you can persuade your local paper to do a feature on you and your work.

Once the word is out there, the bookings will begin, but expect an ooze rather than a deluge. It takes time to penetrate the public consciousness. Be prepared for the fact that some organisations will expect you to have a DBS certificate and public liability insurance.

When somebody asks you to speak, don't forget to check with them the exact date, time and venue, instructions for reaching the venue and parking/public transport arrangements, and the length of time for which they would like you to talk. You need to advise them of three important points:

- the exact nature of your talk, so that everyone knows what to expect. If you are planning to talk about your hilarious experiences in a tent in the Lakes and your audience is expecting to hear how you walked the great wall of China, there's a conflict of interest. And yes, these sort of discrepancies really do arise.
- the fact that you have a book on the theme and will be bringing copies to sell, if that's agreeable. It usually is, but it's a courtesy to check.
- the fee you will charge for the engagement. You may be speaking for an hour, but you will be giving up an evening, you will have had travelling and incidental expenses, and you have already put in a lot of time and effort on preparing the book and the talk. Expect to be paid a fair rate – at least the amount you'd pay any expert for their services, such as a hairdresser, decorator or plumber. Most people will expect to pay you. Some offer to contribute to a charity you support. Some will give you a hearty handshake and a potplant. Be realistic. Five elderly ladies in the minister's vestry aren't going to finance your next trip to the Bahamas, but something towards it acknowledges your professionalism.

When the day comes for your talk, dress smartly, arrive promptly, be lovely to everyone, deliver the speech with panache, answer the questions with charm, and make sure you sell a few books.

When you get home, make a note of the talk you have given and its reception. Think about the parts that went particularly well, and how you could expand upon them. Decide where improvements could be made. Most importantly, jot down any ideas for your next mini-memoir. This is not a flippant suggestion. An audience who laughed at the talk and leapt to buy copies of your book *Life with a Psychotic Cat* might be equally enthusiastic if you came back next year to talk about – and sell – *Ten Years with a Disturbed Dog*.

The good news is that writing mini-memoirs and public speaking feed upon each other. The contents of a mini-memoir can be adapted to fuel a talk, but the contents of a talk are equally fertile ground for adaptation into a new mini-memoir.

The Next Stage

If you have been bitten by the mini-memoir bug, you may find that your next stage is to write another … and another … and another. That's fine. You have proved to yourself that this form of writing is for you, so explore and exploit it by keeping to the same genre, maybe supplementing your writing with public speaking as suggested.

If you want to go further into this type of writing, why not consider attempting the bigger version, expanded and extended to produce a full scale autobiography? Like the mini-memoir, this begins with an assessment of the material to be included and the boundaries you will set.

The difference is in the range of the book. A mini-memoir is a little sample of life, while an autobiography is a bigger deal. The longer work covers a lot more ground, but it still needs to be animated by all the writing skills listed under the Prose Narrative heading in chapter two.

If the idea of tackling the complete autobiography of a much larger chunk of your life seems too great, remember that you can use mini-memoirs as 'staging posts' in the process. If you have written four or five mini-memoirs about different aspects of your childhood, you will be able to adapt and transform them to appear within the autobiography. The dynamics will not be the same because of the very different lengths of the material, but you will have vibrant passages to be embedded into your book. Do remember to make those alterations to the work, though, in fairness to readers who have already bought and read your mini-memoir.

Some people enjoy writing mini-memoirs as much for the size and scale of the book, and the pleasures of self-publication, as for the nature of the content. An interesting departure is to move into different short books. If you think in terms of milestones rather than memories, you will see there is the opportunity for writing in one of the styles listed in chapter two to celebrate the big occasions of life. Some ideas for these include:

- a verse celebration of a wedding, with poems about the courtship, proposal, engagement, service, reception and after.
- a book devoted to a special birthday, with contributions from family and friends, funny stories, photos, factoids and snippets.
- a collage book to celebrate a birth, with information about the baby's arrival, names and their meanings, other things that have happened on the same day in history, Western and Chinese horoscopes, and general information about new babies.
- the birthday of a building. You could write the history of a house, looking at what was there before, the house's construction, former owners, physical changes, changes of use, etc.
- anniversary book, with a look at news reports of the years from marriage to the present, and a parallel look at personal occurrences in the family.
- a local history book, full of fillers and memories, coinciding with a significant anniversary of some feature of the neighbourhood.
- a commonplace book, a compilation of knowledge and information put together scrapbook-style.

In short, any special event can be commemorated in this fashion, and a lasting memory of the occasion will be created.

Whether you are writing a mini-memoir or a milestone book, to be shared in the family or sold around the world, there is one guideline you should never forget. Your task should be a real labour of love, and the whole process should bring you and your readers great pleasure.

Happy writing!